ASH ON WIND

SANDRA BERRIS

MUSE INK PRESS

Muse Ink Press
1465 E. Putnam Avenue, Suite 529
Old Greenwich, CT 06870

First Edition

Printed in the United States of America

ISBN 978-0-9859915-3-1

Cover art reprinted with permission of the artist, Kim Cogan, www.kimcogan.com, "Tree on Noriega," oil on canvas, © 2012.

Designed by Ryan Ratliff

For Brian, Lee and Susan

CONTENTS

1

2

3

1

IF LIGHTS DIM

When you're asked where
were you when Kennedy died,
you remember

and relive those hours and days
of surprise and grief
with déjà vu,

its disagreeable sameness,
so you know what I mean
when I tell you

I remember
the day a mass murderer died;
I remember

and I'm there now
in Lincoln, Nebraska, where
in every room across town

this moment when the switch
is pulled by Everyone,
the lights dim,

a phenomenon
the utility company denies,
but I tell you

the hands of the populace
gripped and pressed Starkweather
into burnt black death

12:01 a.m. that Friday
his shaved head shook
from five separate 2,200-volt charges

3

and he was pronounced dead
as the eleven victims he sent to
darkness during January of 1958

The community had been in electric fear,
count of victims and panic rising
like feet of snow, unstoppable

as a blizzard. I remember
in my eighth grade class
when Mrs. Buckner announced

> *the Ward family has been shot.*
> Sharon's head, hitting typewriter keys—
> *Bing! Bam!*

her low wail spreads
across the room like smoke,
touching all of us

whether we know her boyfriend Mike or not
his parents and maid bringing the total to six,
the fear and darkness as Mrs. Buckner

lowers all of the shades,
tells us *no one*
can go home unescorted,

fathers already arriving
with shotguns and grim faces
hoping to site a shock of red hair,

that bowlegged teen shuffling cowboy boots
in the wrong direction, a fleeing pheasant
rising over a cornfield

for the trigger fingers of hunters
who know easy dinner and just rewards,
sheltering children into Pontiacs and Fords;

paranoia drapes around us,
wondering who's next,
where the red-headed fool and his girl

are driving right now, *maybe
into my garage or yours,
maybe already waiting inside your house*

Lights flicker and dim—
memory explodes!
and I know where I was

What makes you remember?

ATONEMENT

"... it was perverse
for the elderly to outlive the young."
—From Joyce Carol Oates' *Wild Nights*

Yes, perverse.
He would have been 43 this year.
I say *he*. I felt it
From the beginning. The fetus
Curled up like a fetus,
How else? A masculine
Snail-like curl voided
In a bloody gush,
Shameful on a sheet of Charmin.
Unmistaken for any other,
Then released to ethereal waters
To disappear, down, downwards,
The curl inside a curling vortex.
Goodbye. As if he never happened,
Never thought of again. Except
In silence as one
Shivers into shadows, subjects oneself
To the cruelties of what
Can never change. Tonight
I shall throw a party. The best
Wines, gourmet fare, and cake.
No one will know this is belated
For you, nor wonder at who
You might have been, become.
Is it possible one day we may meet
In the heavens? I am
Rehearsing how I'll explain.

OFF-ROAD POEMING

You ride shotgun   I'll drive

After the click of fastened seatbelts
        our poem takes off—

bodies mold against high-backed seats,
a spiral of music rides wind that riffles hair

scenery scrolls in a blur of greens and whites and blues
as we accelerate without restraint

past the corner which we know leads to town

                this is where our poem swerves off
        follows gravel roads through thickets—

no signs, no cops, no other poem in sight—

forging recklessly ahead over obstacles bounding spinning
rubber on stones ice-slick in summer

until the poem is out of control

                spinning words
                applying throttle
                gearing up for an approaching hill

wheels slip on gravel
but the weight of words carries us up and

over the crest where the road turns sharply

left but our poem goes   straight

                        airborne

               and plummets to a ravine below

       lands on all fours, lucky not to roll

at a railroad crossing and a s!top si!gn

where we hurtle back in time to a drag race years ago—

       broken glass

           broken bodies

              brOken gLASS

who can explain physics and aerodynamics
how a girl
hurtles through space in an orbit of shards—
the head stopped by a sign below

                  the body where
a train crosses each night
and whistles, whistles

as a cloud of dust
        rises
           obstructs the view
                suspends

BALLOON

Only one woman shares the emergency waiting room with us.
Her gray hair rides like a small animal on her head.
Her eyes do not meet mine. She looks past us
or through us and I study her
in her flowered cotton dress and sensible shoes.
Then a man enters the room and approaches her
speaking in secrets, a whisper of *Reverend*
reaching my ears. My neck hairs rise.
He guides her out of the waiting room,
her tremulous bulk in a frightening quiver.
Soon it is our turn to pass through the double doors,
talk to the physician treating our daughter's injured leg.
Beyond an open curtain
a young boy, perhaps eight or nine, lies
lifeless on a gurney. Doctors and nurses stand useless.
My whisper *what's happened*
thunders hushed air.
He has aspirated a red balloon, his favorite color,
from the bag of afternoon amusement,
the simple toy flying inward, flinging
his soul somewhere else,
the tracheotomy bringing forth
only silence, blood-red.
I glimpse the old woman, the grandmother I'm told,
watching the boy while his parents travel abroad.
She is a wattle of arms in a storm. Her whole body
shakes like some great tree giving up precious fruit.

BURN

My Aunt Cecilia was burned
when she fried scrambled eggs in an old iron pan
and fainted—weak from a three-day bout of flu—
a faint face-first into fire.

She came to with her torso aflame,
so she rolled over her kitchen floor
spinning like a golden tin angel
that twirls from heat of a candle.

Her glasses melted, but her vision spared.
She stood before the bathroom mirror
focusing—first her pink nightgown,
a blackened fragment like fear,

then her chest and face,
black marshmallows.
My Uncle John found her sitting in a cold
tub, her silent mouth a scorched "O".

Six weeks later, still in the burn unit,
she told Uncle John *Rosie keeps calling.*
Her sister Rosie, buried in Chicago
years ago. So John whispered *It's alright, go.*

And while his words echoed,
Aunt Cecilia exhaled her last breath.
Within that hour, while relatives
comforted Uncle John, I tiptoed close

to encounter death. Spellbound
by her bandaged head, the nose
gone, and most of the right ear
now a delicate black crust

like burnt snowflake cookies
that crumble when touched,
I pulled back the white sheet to
an absence of skin on her chest,

winding strips of exposed muscle,
dull twisted cords, textbook perfect,
and I knew Aunt Cecilia was somewhere else.
Life is not this real.

PETER

In memory of Peter Bataille

Eleven only,
sprawling shoots for legs,
he let the air uproot him
into the path of that oncoming van,
while he waved to his friends
who watched
from the windows of a bus,
moving their lives and his
in opposite directions.

The surgeon tried
to reconstruct his frame, inflated
his lungs with false hope,
but he was still
cold, inanimate.

I see him
cross my thoughts from the west at dusk
and remember his smile, the same one
with closed curved lips he wore
Sundays as the altar boy.

Now the earth is hard, crazed
from summer sun. One red geranium
survives the heat above his head.
I do not mourn. He is not there.
He is the sparkle of light
caught in the branches of evergreen.

AN INTIMACY OF MATTER

" . . . Then I will go back
to that silent evening, when the past just managed
to overlap the future, if only by a trace,
and the light doubles and shines
through the dark the sparkling that heavens the earth."
—Galway Kinnell, *That Silent Evening*

I know the sparkling that heavens the earth,
we saw it,
more than that, bore witness to strange phenomenon:
together on the edge of lawn this November day standing in a half-circle
of four, while Lee, eldest daughter, on the end
of our blood-bonded curve,
scoops her hand into ashes and tiny bones
kept dark and airless for nearly a year, the remains
of our beloved terrier, creature in a black canister of tin
patterned with hand-painted orange and pink flowers,
keeper of earthly remains,
and like a brain sifting memories
her hand gathers sorrow
and rises like a tree and opens
in loving gesture as if a wave
releasing ash to wind,
her hand empty now
as we each take turns touching the past, releasing fragments
of frenzied laps around the house,
the singing along with an alto sax,
the sitting in sun-slants across the hardwood floor,
the spinning in dance for a crumb,
until the final handful of all that was and is
floats on wind and at this precise moment
we see heaven's sparkle,
dormant ash on air, magic dust, flashing like snow and stars and also
at this precise moment
all the neighbors' dogs begin barking,
their conundrum catching our startled belief.

REVERSALS

We turn the soil, hard and dark
from winterkill, unearthing worms

pebbles, weeds. Scoop out

small wells to fill with peat moss,
tapping each root pod from its plastic pot

snugging them in with dirt, mulch,
and a trickle of water.

Grateful, we stand back to admire

our babies in the garden—
reds, pinks, petals of purple.

Then do the usual Saturday stuff

trekking to town on errands.
We return late afternoon

to look in on our darling dahlias

shockingly gone, beheaded!
And whistling over the stone wall

a large, damnable woodchuck

diving into its burrow
with scant interest in abundant clover

our dahlias plucked one by one.

We drive to the hardware store to buy
a trap with two metal doors

each set to snap shut

when the rodent weighs in on the middle platform,
a lever, really, laded with bait:

first lettuce, tried to no avail; next

a sprinkle of fragrant vanilla; then chunks
of apples and berries, string beans and corn,

peaches and melon; peas; and weeks later—

a trapper's bullet aimed from a hedgerow.
Our garden flooding with grief and guilt,

the gentle fellow, still as a stick.

LAMENT

Tragedy should move one
"by pity and terror."
—Aristotle, *Poetics*

The turkey thinks I am wild

its wide eye catches me in the window glass
before the bird takes off

a running start like pole vaulting
accelerating across grass,
the lift off
a slow rising
cumbersome
as a 757 or the wooden Spruce Goose

                It roosts
in a tall oak, where the edge of yard
falls into woods

Bewitched like Narcissus, each morning
the bird returns to find
its own display of fanned tail feathers

the naïve bird lured and blinded
                   by an elusive mate
that prunes its plume in mimicry,
luster bouncing off glass

Afternoons
it struts in a thicket of grass,
peck-pecking for insects, insatiable

head bobbing forward
             leading a parade of plump brown feathers

Then today, a loose trail of iridescence
drifts across lawn and I can only wonder

what bow and arrow, what fox or coyote . . .

    symmetry of terror in wide-eye reflection

    and the molted grief

        of how the self deceives.

SPENCER

Is sniffing his way through the yard,
sniffing his way to a hornet's hole,

tail flapping, ears abuzz
with something other than that which comes

in an instant, the sharp stingers
stuck inside his nose, his body

atremble as if called forth on Judgment Day
aware of so many scattered birds, the mouse

trapped in a woodpile, and whenever possible
cake swooped off the kitchen counter.

Against a quiver of black and white fur
his tail tucks in like the latch of a door.

How does one comfort the injured?
Set right what simply happens?

This is the nature of silence:
he lies down at our feet

awaiting a long, smooth, repetitive stroke
that soothes and surely speaks.

DOG AND CAT IN BED

For Susan

A mother listens to CNN. Another bomb
has exploded. Another terrorist in Paris
has had his say, his words like a rabid dog,
an explosive monologue of flying hex nuts
spinning through the car of a commuter train
slicing off feet like stems of mushrooms from passengers.

Her daughter is one of the daily passengers
riding the Metro to classes in spite of a bomb,
traveling weekends to distant cities by train.
The mother worries about her daughter in Paris,
the odds of involvement in random acts, a string of hex nuts
now a rosary of preoccupation. She ignores her dog.

She imagines her daughter slipping out of sight like the dog
down the foreign streets, a passenger
injected into the mainstream of the city, hex nuts
exploding arteries that take her with the bomb
every direction along with the other Paris
commuters clothed in black on the train.

When the daughter calls home she tells of the train
regulars: a woman with nits in her hair who with her dog
garishly begs for a living and makes a student feel rich in Paris;
and she tells of Birdman, another of the passengers,
who flaps his arms toward passersby and flits like a bomb
in a harmless but harried manner like a hexed nut;

and she tells of the harpist, another hexed nut,
who plucks out Bach and sings along on the train
so that her begging performance is a bomb
compared to the endearing spectacle of a cat and a dog
who nestle together in a doll's bed as passengers
under a tiny blanket for which a beggar collects Paris

coins. "I'll send you their picture from Paris,"
the daughter tells her mother, distracted from hex nuts,
imagining the surprised faces of passengers
watching the compassionate, joyful beggar on the train
who plays his accordion music near the sleeping dog
and cat, his pride exploding like a bomb.

The mother momentarily forgets the bombs in Paris
spinning hex nuts and smiles thinking of the dog
and cat cozy under a blanket, sleeping on the train as passengers.

TO THE BURGLAR

Do you ever wonder what you left behind?

Your glove prints marking the wall,
frantic love pats searching for switches,

maybe you, too, intimated by the dark,
those smears and shadows now painted over;

and that mud-slicked log I found
surrounded by shattered glass

from the sliding door bashed in that night,
late June; and the one simply fun

faux-gold earring shaped like a faucet,
the spout dripping water of pearl

that you dropped on the driveway
in hasty retreat, the alarm shouting

like some angry drunk; and my father's
gold cufflinks worth the moon

beside a tarnished stellate ring overlooked
in a box on a shelf in the closet;

and smudged prints in cop dust
sprinkled across the floor like salt in wounds.

Had I been home, would you have been
fearless, cool in my face, unflinching

or turned about in the dark
the shadow of intent stolen from you?

In my dreams the veracity of crime
ghost walks in my brain, a memory scar

white with fright, some asexual rape,
mouth agape. You, coward and crook,

who can't hold a candle to Procrustes.
Dare you come back, let's see how you measure up.

AMULET

At least let me give you the foot of a hare,
an amulet of good luck to charm away evil

or perhaps a four-leaf clover
would suffice to reverse your fortune

or maybe I could hang a horseshoe
above your bedroom door, though you tell me

you are not superstitious, you don't believe
in old wives' tales, witches on brooms, magic,

customs that smack of tall tale,
that you'd even stare down an evil eye,

and you open umbrellas indoors and have never
suffered from triskaidekaphobia

as you pull out a dollar bill and push your luck
with 13 stars, 13 arrows, 13 leaves with 13 berries.

I'm sure I saw you last week walk under a ladder,
though I admit I was distracted by stepping over a crack

before I ducked inside the coffee shop
when a black cat crisscrossed near the corner.

Coincidence, you say, but I'll bet more than once
that you've crossed your fingers behind your back

and tonight when the stars come out
you might even make a wish

while I knock on wood for you
and spill a little salt over my left shoulder.

2

VESTIGE

For Walter

They never gave her back the man they took.

She knew that right away. He won't talk

about what he saw, what he did,

but holds it in, knife-painful.

All the shit of war flows through his arteries.

He doesn't want to talk about it, though

once he told about a chicken, the surprise

of silly bird strut across a rice field.

Bar-be-QUE! said a soldier, so

they set down the chopper. His friend

jumped out in comic strut and sprint.

The guys all laughing.

Then they saw chicken and man

blown to bits. Smaller than anything

cut in a Cuisinart. Gone. *For a Goddam chicken.*

And once he told of a beautiful prostitute.

Long black hair, tiny features, terrific figure.

And her odd webbed feet from always walking

barefoot, toes splayed across the sand.

But that's it. Tiny feathers

still stick to his skin, get up his nose.

LETTER TO CAMBODIAN FACES

While I listened to the Beatles,
smoked pot, protested war,
read Rimbaud and Baudelaire,

you, on another continent,
sons and daughters of intellects,
of educators, children of entrepreneurs

endured shackles
that replaced your school desks.
And the guillotine with draining buckets

transformed your playing field.
I confess to winning the birth lottery
while your confession

of guilt by birth
they pried out with whips,
or a metal vise tightening on the brain,

or for the most resistant
the long-necked glass bottle
which my imagination can only

speculate what horror, these tools
now on display at Tuol Sleng
for tourists like myself to contemplate.

Your faces, not forgotten, remain
imprisoned at S-21, where we gaze at eyes
wide with fear and startle

at those few faces unaware
of Comrade Duch's intentions,
who smiled at the camera.

LIKE HEAT FROM STONE

Decades later the brain hears

      shovels scraping soil, digging trenches,

      Cambodians forced to dig

      their own shallow graves.

Loud, piped-in music blasts

      over screams, beatings, gunshot,

      thuds of infants

      flung like baseball bats against trees.

From the dusty paths one treads today

      the past pushes up through soil—

      scraps of fabric: someone's shirt,

      a woman's scarf, a child's pants

and countless bits of bones—

      a vanished generation rising.

HANDS

"Prosper the work of our hands for us!"
——Psalm 90:17

Distinguish us from animals
The brilliant design of opposable
Thumbs allowing us to grasp and pinch
And lift a tiny thread, a spoon, or
Handfuls of whatever is in reach.

A simple movement
Of wrist and graceful fingers
Beckoning. Hands with their own
Alphabet. Without words pulling
You toward me, hands

Sharing love, a soft caress.
Now I press my palms together,
Thumbs like two sentries beneath
Polished curves of nail, the tall
Index pair tapping.

The remaining fingers link
So my hands resemble a tiny chapel
Where I now give thanks. I pray for all
Those courageous who exist without
Hands, devoured

By machinery or left behind in war
Or hacked off by rebels, all those
Who can no longer grasp or craft
Or work or write or offer a simple
Handshake to set things right.

POEM WRITTEN
IN RAIN AND DRUNKENNESS

Please excuse me Xu We, for stealing your title.
I'm certain no one remembers it from the 1500s

and it works just as well today, here, as it did
for you in China. You must know how I feel as

I stand in the rain waiting for a taxi after dinner,
though for you I'm sure it was a rickshaw. And

the memory of three glasses of wine still on my lips,
such pleasure shared throughout the ages!

I am delighted to learn that *hao shi* means
"a fine thing indeed" in Chinese, so the sneeze

coming on from this dampness bodes well. I know
the Chinese have 100 ways to say happiness. Surely

I have as many, but for tonight, it is just this one
of writing a poem here, in drunkenness, in the rain.

CIRCLES

O

Sociologists say if you know five people
You know everyone in the world.
I haven't met the right five people.
I'm missing whole continents.

O

A circle looks closed from the outside.
I'll jump in the middle.
Sink to the bottom or rise to the top,
Outside I can only look in.

O

Don't believe it.
All are not equal from the center of a circle.
The ring is closed.
But expands under influence.

O

Play the game. Who Do You Know?
Pieces of friends lay on the board.
Pick them up.
Hide some in your pocket. Wear one on your lapel.

O

Circles are magic.
I keep rising from the middle
Like a rabbit from a hat.
The imagination of others is greater than I.

O

I tried to disappear
In Chinatown once,
Follow an uncertain forecast
From a fortune cookie,
Cross a street
At a dangerous diagonal.
I met myself on the other side.

O

Everything revolves.
I'm back where I began
Looking for the right five people.

KRABLOONIK RESTAURANT

Something howls

a lonesome call
resonating Russian winters.

We descend snow and ice layers
cut in the side of Snowmass
and think
of the return:
these steep wooden stairs.

But the peaks of A-frames
draw us deeper, closer
to find
the sled dogs, each
chained to a hut
to keep them safe
or us,
their eyes
cerulean blue
piercing the night sky.

Inside we order wild
mushroom soup and caribou,
partridge, buffalo or pheasant,
each dish different from each other's
and from any before.

We leave the warm wood hum
of the log cabin
where outside, the owner

tries to hush
the hollow Husky cry
that winds up the trail
and wraps us like smoke.

In the dark
we retrace our steps,
penetrate
a closed trail to the past
that the sharp knife
of the howl strikes.

NO RETURN

At Pioneer Park I search for the giant swings
where once I flew with the eagle
and found the secrets of Indians.

I reach the chain link barrier where
an honest herd grazed on the short grass
of the plains that went forever to my young eyes.

I knew if I climbed over that ten-foot barrier
and followed the buffalo I could find
the edge of the world.

Today I see two: scraggly, dusty,
hunched over they look weak.
I turn my back and walk up the rock-imbedded hill

where a statue kneels, fanning his fire
with a metal blanket. I look skyward
for messages but only see clouds.

TRAVELER

I long for California and 70 degrees,
pick hot green chiles and cans of tomato
sauce from the cupboard, arrange each
on the Formica square
as though packing a suitcase.

To flour tortillas, round
suns on the pan, I add hot
cayenne and jalapeno. I want
flan, but settle for Jell-O
Instant Pudding, butterscotch.

Later I move toward Bradshaw's
"Bright Beginnings," its intense
watercolor reds and oranges my horizon
where I lie on the sandy colored couch
and dream of reading poetry about
silken gowns, lifting, blowing.

Blowing snow hits the front window
and eaves pop,
resettle,
unsettling me.

I plan for Florida tomorrow
via large, Atlantic shrimp,
unshelled, cooked in water flavored
with garlic, and something
orangey for dessert, a chiffon pie,
light and airy.

I pencil in Thursday's chicken,
whole, eager for the wishbone.

DRIVING IN WALES, EARLY SPRING

A day of apricity, sheep lounge like picnickers in spring green pastures.
Only yesterday, they hid from rain, looking like white garbage sacks

Lining the hedge-rows. A wet wool scent beyond daffodils. Today
White rumpled lambs stand on new legs, still as toys placed within meadows.

The narrow road winds through woodland, dense with beech and oak.
Trunks and branches, the green haze of buds still revealing distant hills.

In a few weeks, this road will tunnel under canopies obstructing the view.
A stretch near a hunting club is dotted with fallen, still pheasants, striated

Feathers of black, rust and gold still aloft in the breeze, birds never to make it
To fall feasts. We stop for fortification of noontime pork belly, beer, a bit of

Salmon and trout, then drive onward past signs unpronounceable along
The River Wye where a red kite flies overhead, sailing its rust-red forked tail.

We think of Wordsworth and Turner when we stop in Tintern,
Those sensations sweet in lonely rooms or fixed upon a canvas.

Our intake of breath astonished by the massive ruins of the Abbey
Set against a wooded hillside. The stone shell sparks imagination

Of invisible monks passing through doorways, their brown cloaks
Blending into the mottled greys and golds of the courtyard rocks,

Their rounded shoulders as they gather around the single monastery fire,
Their silent passage through soaring arches to genuflect to a statue

Of Virgin Mary and Child. All ghosts from more than 700 years ago.
The past hinged to the present as cameras click on towering stone and lichen.

DIFFERENT DREAMS

Drawn to the pueblo like smoke to an opening
She returns to the dusty trails
Of a fortress, one thousand years old.

With midnight eyes, somber hair
Clasped tight at the nape of her long slender neck,
Half-Navajo, half-Sioux, she lopes

Past old women who squat
On stoops of small adobes, their soot-black eyes
Seeking buyers of silver, moccasins, pottery, drums.

She is our guide, a recent college graduate,
Who works in town as a secretary but
On weekends gives tours of the Pueblo.

We follow her past a crumbled wall where
Wooden crosses lean. *Remnants*, she tells us,
Of the conquering Spanish, from re-used graves.

No matter, she says, a procession of tourists
Hanging on her words, *Navajo's bodies
Return to earth and dissolve into dust.*

We enter a small chapel where
At the altar, a single casket holds Jesus,
A statue who lies in state forever

Jesus perpetually laden with flowers
Surrounded by female statues
Clothed in the green satin symbolic of Mother Earth.

Saints dressed by seasons—green, blue, yellow, white—
Stand guard by each pew where she finally says,
I am Catholic by habit. No pun intended.

I worship the earth. Outside she kneels above a chamber
Carved in the depths of the soil. Her red finger,
Soil-stained like Spanish blood, points

To a chamber below, where in a privileged ceremony,
She will be wrapped in the damp scent of earth.
This is my dream, she says, *that one day I will be*

The first female governor of the Navajos, the one who will remove
All tourists from this sacred ground, who will empty
The corral of automobiles, who will never trust what I cannot control.

Heavy gusts stir up more red soil. Navajo dust.
Navajo remains. Navajo dreams.
But for now, she says, *I return each night to this reservation,*

Lug water, two bucketsful, up the ladder propped against the adobe wall,
Worry about dents in my clay rooftop from high heels,
Touch the hem of night before descending below.

Inside, a cauldron hangs over heating coals,
Boils to heat a flat iron to press her one white blouse.
In flickering light she reads by propane lamp,

Despises her brothers who eat food of the white man,
Despises those who live in HUD prefab houses with water
And electricity, despises those who watch TV and listen

To suggestive music. Lost now in thought, her dreamy face
Mystical, she tells us how she fishes in the lake,
Hunts for deer and elk, plants squash and beans and corn,

Here, on this once sacred ground. Heavy gusts blow red soil
Into our ears, up our nostrils, our eyes
Blinking out grains of Navajo dust, Navajo dreams.

ANY SATURDAY AFTERNOON IN IOWA

"Stuart is home to 1500 good eggs
plus a few stinkers," boasts the Chamber of Commerce.

For cash terms Elvira Lewis will sell you her food market.
Anyone with need for a one story 15' x 75' building

with natural gas and good roof can give her
20% down on the day of sale and the balance

on showing merchantable. For good measure
she'll throw in the antique meat block and two meat saws;

she might even throw in the wooden storm windows
and the spade and snow shovels. The rest of the fixtures

and equipment such as a new 36" pilferage reflector mirror,
a sanitary meat scale, a national adding machine, meat knives,

a dairy clock, a large fan, and the inventory ranging
from Dixie cups to men's underwear to

"more items too numerous to mention" are up for auction.
The clerks and auctioneer will be ready.

Her competition is down the block at the auction
for Duane Kraft. He is selling a mess of antiques:

97 Winchester Pump 12 gauge Shot Gun, 4570 Grass Rifle
with a walnut stock, antique lamps, a copper boiler,

an oak pilot wheel off a ship, tobacco tins,
and a Wurlitzer Record player—"this thing really works."

Folks may come to Stuart from Menlo or far away as Greenfield
when word travels down the back roads like tumbleweeds.

POSTCARD FROM HARBOUR ISLAND, BAHAMAS

Dear Flo,
Beautiful pink sand.
Turquoise sea. Pin
prick marks my room.
I have no space to
tell you . . .

. . . of palms that rise and float,
tethered in constant breeze,
or of beach dotted with shells
and fragments of lowly creatures,
a hue of seasonings. Waves
in their endless tidal clock
sweep seaweed across my path,
black fingers reaching for shore
from oil spills far out at sea.
Blue-green lizards, a ruler's length each,
dart across narrow jungle paths
over coral lumps in limestone soil
and disappear in density
where rat snakes coil.

Preston, the boat boy, skin black
and lizard-bumpy, flashes
motorboat skill, white teeth in the sun,
teases and tests me at the dock,
walks like a blackbird on narrow ridges
of a boat before skimming beneath the pier
to bring over the rig. *Say Bah-ee,*
he instructs. *No problem,* I answer.

Bahamian women sell baskets
from wooden flapboard stands,
the mats and hats dotting the decks
of yachts floating near yellow buoys,
a boast of American flags above
polished brass and mahogany fishing chairs.

Inside the Manor House I cool my feet
on shiny terracotta and blue tiles
scrubbed daily by Jane. Her glazed eye
looks past me, her good eye burns
through me. The other cottage cleaners,
invisible as the snakes, make beds
and bring fresh linens smooth
as daylight easing
into a purple rim across the bay.

In the full-length mirror
I gauge suntan to select
one hibiscus of orange, pink, yellow or red
that lies on each table like forgotten hats.

Over cocktails, strangers become family
who tell of a shark off the main pier, a sleek
barracuda circling the dock, a finless waterski,
scraped arm, sprained finger, a picnic lunch
on Mann Island, sand dollars in the sea-foamed
edge of beach, and the definition of *diphyallic terata*
from last night's game of "Trivial Pursuit."

The Club's small white van bounces and bumps
over the one rutted dirt road to Dunmore Town,
as sudden toots from a faulty horn
a noisy farewell and unexpected hello
from those traveling to town, and I
imagine the clouds of mauve dust rising
with each thrum of engine as I watch
the tiniest and fastest variety of ants
share our sugar bowl and linger on the table
long after the last bottle of wine is finished.

In my room the fireplace
framed by black tiles and dark wood,
two watercolors, a boat dock and harbour house,
over twin beds, the white nubby spreads mimicking
white stucco walls, so stark
against the dark wood of everything else,
I think of Jane as the generator's
intermittent hum, lights dimming and surging,
lulls me to sleep . . . .

                    Tomorrow
after French toast and omelets
I must board the taxi boat to Eleuthra to fly home.
Beyond the boatman's kinks, like tiny knots
of needlepoint in rows, I will see
the stone walkway lined with coconut palms
grow smaller and watch until
the paradise of flowers disappears,
these days sloughed, cell by cell,
to winter-white skin.

COSTA RICAN ECLOGUE

i.

A mixture of sifted soil, a shimmer of golden light.
Velvet skin. How we want to reach out and touch.
Read skin like Braille and linger. A silky, fleshy feel.

If sunset shouts romance, surely skin tolls tiny bells.
Tongues shepherd us to soft hills and contours of other.

ii.

Something sensual, the long hanging nests of orioles.

Ficus trees like wide umbrellas shading reclining cows.
Songbirds silent. Tiny birds

Riding on the backs of Brahmin bulls. Bony cutouts.
Cows the color of dust. Some will not survive the length of heat.

Others will be slaughtered. Egrets roosting on leafless trees
appear as blossoms of white flowers.

iii.

Only the head of a crocodile. Behold and beware.

Its cataracted eye. Several feet of spiky tail
floats like a log in the canal. Our boat moves closer.

Basilisk, a lizard walking upon water reaches shore.
Jesucristo.

In camouflage of branch, above raffia-lined shores,
iguanas spread long claws.

White-faced monkeys woof like dogs, swinging
from branch to branch above mangroves and marsh.

The babies ride their mothers' black furry backs as if
Velcroed, oblivious to hummingbirds and hawks.

iv.

A long spine down the middle of the country.

300 dormant volcanoes. 10 active. One shooting sparks.
When an earthquake comes, we awaken shaking.

The room trembling like a frightened goat. Who rattles
my door at this hour? Who shuttles a clanging cart?

Bedsprings and door creaking, a cacophony
of nighttime music, of shifting tectonic plates.

Our nightmare, but only night terrors for natives.
They don't remember earth's ruptures and rebounds.

v.

In a van passing rows and rows of one-room shacks.

A TV colors each doorway or window like a bouquet
mismatched to impoverished surroundings. Screens and bars.

Fences crying, Keep out! as Nicaraguans cross this border
for what is greener. For long hours in fields

of sugar cane and rice. Tilapia farms. Papayas, bananas,
mangoes, plantains, melons.

vi.

The air is hot
         We wear flip-flops
                  Across the bridge
                           Above the pool
                                    The bridge an arch
                                             O Dragonfly
                                    Peninsula slung
                           Between two wings
                  Of bay that's blue
         And sea so cool
The air is hot!

NEVIS NARRATIVE

Imagine this   A tiny island   Late afternoon
Your goats have not come home

      Playful goats like school children
              Ambling
              Single file
              Along
              The dirt road

     Jumping up
            On narrow stone walls to taste
              Fragrant flowers

But today your goats do not return

So you go up the mountain
           In search of what is yours

And while you are gone
           A volcano erupts somewhere in the world

And a tidal wave
           Embraces your village and won't let go

You come back down the mountain
           And everyone is gone

You have your goats
           But you cannot imagine.

HOLY MACKEREL

For Jean

Blessed be the pilot-fish,
naucrates ductor,

sacred fish of sailors,
showing the way.

In camouflage
of dark blue bands

traversing their bodies,
they glide

through dark seas,
a silent covert course

companion to sharks
amidst weeds and driftwood.

In white foam of open sea
they spawn transparent

nearly invisible eggs
that float like thoughts

ready to hatch
across a blank page

this one long dialogue of heart:
words connected and rearranged

mine, yours, and all
the poets before us.

THIRTEEN WAYS OF LOOKING AT THE SEA

I.

All along the shore
The sea drifts in and out,
The moon pulling the sea, the sea pulling me.

II.

Three sensations at once:
Scent of salt and kelp.
Sight of spindrift's dance,
Sound of churning waves.

III.

The sea whirls onto sand,
Always an interrupter.

IV.

A fish and the sea
Are one.
A fish and the sea and we
Are one.

V.

I do not know which to prefer,
The tide coming in or going out.
Does it matter?
I am infused with joy and calm.

VI.

Long dark fingers shadow the sand.
Is this where the world will end
Under the horizon's curve
Of golden light?

VII.

A pirate ship of clouds
Looms on the horizon.
Dusky figures recede from the beach
Like hawks circling and reaching their nests
Just before dark.

VIII.

I know that this is a paradise
Of majestic making.
I know too that my soul
Sings with the knowing.

IX.

Birds silhouette
And anchor the shore
Until freedom of flight.

X.

In a tangle like driftwood
A man and woman rise and fall like waves
Under a quilt on the beach.

XI.

The town slants into the sea
And the sea sifts it back.
Ribs of driftwood settle on sand
And shadows splash beneath a throat of pines.

XII.

The sea ignites in apricots and pinks.
The sun flares blood orange
Then sinks into lavender hues
Until night air cools
And blackens the sea.

XIII.

Mist drips and drizzles
As fog devours the bay.
The invisible sea breathes in and out
Unable to conceal its presence.

CARMEL BY THE SEA

After Neruda; for Caron

I do not want to be a tourist in Carmel by the Sea
walking down Ocean Avenue, peering into shops.

I do not want to stroll on the beach
following my dog, watching him bound into surf.

I do not want to picnic on a bench
sipping wine, eating a Deli sandwich.

And never do I want to marry on the beach,
vows shouted over wind ruffling hair.

No, I want to live forever here in paradise
feeling the immensity of nature.

I want to watch the sun rise each day
and sparkle on the waves,

And later watch the sun set
draping soft sherbet colors across the sea

Or igniting the sky with flames
or sharing a singular flash of green eyelid.

Here I am nothing. A speck
standing on the beach.

Replaceable. Insignificant. A speck
spotting a dolphin, then a whale, a flotilla of birds.

All my troubles wash away
glittering into the sea.

How can anything matter when here
in Carmel by the Sea the world alone is immense.

3

SNAKE LOVE

Mother warned me
if I was naughty
a snake
a long, black snake
would rise up
from the toilet
so I'd press
my knees together to pee
and peer behind me
into the porcelain bowl
an oval sea
of coy words
sharp
like a snap
of belt across flesh
learned from her mother
and her mother before
a cunning snake love
twisting through dreams
like a rising fever
of strange reward.

ONION EVENINGS

I smell onions browning

and our old white frame
house reappears like a puff
of flour dusting the air,
its gray shingled roof muted
by bright shutters added,
her solution for zest.

This night my child interrupts
as I prepare the soup.
I spill flour, and add
too much sherry. I am startled
to hear an old woman
speak through my lips. "Don't
bother me when I'm cooking."

REPRISAL: *"THE KNIVES AND THE HERRING"*

My parents were heterosexual yet unconventional
Their words were knives: his sharp

Sarcasm to his wife; hers, blunt
Outbursts of foul rage. Obedient pots of stew,

Sage-seasoned roasts, dutiful mashed potatoes, a daily façade
Implicit amidst their discord, their discontent.

There was no opportunity to embark on
Voyage or escape. Religious marriage vows were

Binding. God's will. Every Thursday morning, one hour
At dawn, he prayed in Perpetual Adoration,

A society of the church, to where he walked
In half-light. Who knows what he prayed for, what was

Never answered. The red herring, content and docile,
I emerged from a fractious house of violent scenes

Reconciled, petty humiliations ignored.
This hell season, a bore. So much more beyond

Our doorway. And in the end, after fifty years
When she, confined to a ward, thrived in Alzheimer's

Clean slate, he never bothered to visit her. Nor
Spoke her name, not once. Love accommodates.

WHEN I FORGOT TO KNOCK
BEFORE ENTERING THEIR MASTER BEDROOM

Why is it one can deliver fellatio,
      Relish cunnilingus, contort
Into every imaginable position
      And yet cannot, no never ever,
Envision your own parents
      Having sex? I shudder,
Shut my full-moon eyes,
      Plug the cochlea, hum
A jazz rendition of "Jesus Loves Me"
      And entertain the possibility
Remote as Pluto
      While I back step out the door
That maybe, an outside chance,
      I am adopted.

"A FIGURE FOR THE PART"

—From Louise Gluck's "Matins"

Her nightie
raises off her hips,
his two fingers
search for her spot.
She's awakened at dawn
and becomes
a tree
with woodpecker,
repetitive thrusts
making her arch
as if strong wind
curls her limbs.
The bird
satisfied
leaves
while
she is
still
a tree
waiting
for purity of rain,
the warmth of morning sun.

OF TWO MINDS

She calls me
exaggerator
       says that's not
       what she remembers.

Isn't alteration
like paint I say
       added to a canvas?

Some images
are indelible, a rabbit's
       wild swivel struggle
       but hind end smashed.

Others, sweet changelings,
a bar of Fels Naptha soap,
       retro, distorted bubbles.

Those unpredictable leaps
into the past,
       the best of imperfect memory.

MASTERING THE MRI

I tell mother to lie still as an opossum,
count the number of minutes
she can go without swallowing,
how long she can suppress the urge
to kick and hack her way out of say,
a wooden coffin, like Uma Thurman
clawing up breathlessly on film
through depths of freshly turned soil.

Adrift on a noisy boat, pass
under a stone-white ledge.
Irregular *thrum* of engine
offers no promise to get ashore.

Travel incognito.
Cavities and bony structures
seduced by magnetic power
vibrate in echo of strong *tap,
knock, tap tapping.*

        Imagine
what the MRI sees, some likeness
of the interior, hidden alleys and channels
where one could get lost.

THE CLOCK SHOE

Mother can't remember who I am,
talks in riddles, shifts place
and time mid-sentence.

Her body looks the same, her face
under a tent of tidy gray hair,
sweet, alert, yet wild-eyed.

Of the memories we shared
and used to laugh about
I have my half only.

She thinks she's in trouble
with *her* mother for staying out too late
with a girlfriend, both long dead.

Today when I visit Mother
she opens the door a crack.
She calls me aside to ask,

"*Who* is that man?
He's very nice, and I don't
want to hurt his feelings,"

as she points to my father,
"but I really *must* have him leave now."
They've been wed for fifty years.

I give her that simple Alzheimer's test, the task
of drawing a clock face with paper and pencil,
but she ponders, "Hmm, a clock?"

and stalls. "I could draw a violin."
A clock sits on the table in front of her
and she deftly draws a shoe. "A clock shoe,"

we laugh and begin a new set of memories
that will last her only for minutes.

REVELATION

Startled by his bare foot
hidden all these years
beneath black socks, I look
at my father's bone whiteness
standing on a dark braided rug,
see his slender toes, their fragile
grip on his world, and a large
angular bunion, a secret burden
he's pressed beneath him
for much of eighty-five years.

He has asked me to help him—
something he's never asked before—
to clip his split nail that keeps snagging,
like memory, on tiny threads.

I am motionless,
lost in the whiteness of this foot.

HARD WIRED

Poor rabbit,
its hind quarters

flattened by a car,
paws pavement

swivels its head
frantic to see

what's holding it back.

My thoughts jolt
to my father

who lay so small
in hospital sheets,

a breathing tube
threading air near his face

his hand in gesture, tugging.

THE LOGIC OF SNOW

1.

Two weeks ago, at night, she walked out
Through an emergency exit at the end of a corridor,
An exit where the door clicks shut, for security.

Her knobby arthritic fingers touch metal
Mutton bars on the window, not feeling the cold,
Pushing out her 5'2" frame confident as any.

Her cloudy brain talks to her,
        Shall I play golf today? Go the full
18 holes? Yes, I think I can. And she walks

Coatless, oblivious to January temperature,
In blue satin slippers, over ice and snow,
Past thick gray mounds that shovels and plows

Cleared, her brain
Lighting her stroll with sunshine and white roses
And a wide fairway stretching toward the eighteenth green.

*

Collapsed on the cold walkway, face smashed,
Her heart protests and shuts down.
She revives through CPR.

*

An alternate image springs forth:
Frozen bile on sunken lips, her false teeth
Forever smiling in a glass of water.

2.

Ice keeps the swelling down. Bruised
Nose and black eyes. I kiss my mother
On puffy purple and yellow cheeks.

*

I didn't know you were coming, she says.

Her hands press down over my breasts, firm
Strokes running from shoulder to waist.
        Let me feel that wool, she says coyly,
I can teach this man a trick or two
As she turns toward Daddy, who rises
From his reading chair like a ghost.

        Let's go for a walk, Mother grabs my hand.
First you must get dressed, I respond
Holding her inside her room, blocking the door.

        I can go like this, she insists, smoothes
Her blue velour robe, flaps the wrap belt,
Looks down at her wedge slippers.

Let's have coffee, I say,
And she is back at the beginning saying,

        I didn't know you were coming.

3.

I kiss my father as a nurse enters to announce lunch.
Care giving is dragging Daddy down,
Down to disapproval and shaking head.

Have a nice trip, Mother says to the nurse.

We all go on a trip to lunch. Down the corridor
To the dining hall. Most chairs already occupied.

Help, help, help, help . . . over and over
One woman says. Her ship is not sinking.
The room in not aflame. She sits
Calmly at the table uttering only one word.

Where are we going? says Mother
As I help her into her chair at the table where an orderly
Sets a tray of ham, mashed potatoes, Jell-O and peas.

On a cruise ship, I tell her.

4.

While Mother naps, Daddy asks, Where is my car?

He sits in his overstuffed chair,
Newspaper in hand. Nebraska Cornhusker
Red flannel shirt, gray wool trousers. Salt and pepper
Hair belying age. Mind sharp, but body
Slowed, satisfaction stolen from gardening and golf.

We took his keys the same day we moved
Mother and Daddy here. Their house
Of the last forty years, now money
In a checking account. The Power of Attorney
With blessings, long before senility arrived
As the unwanted guest who refuses to leave.

Daddy, trapped like an animal, paces
The perimeter of Room 206.
When am I getting my car?

We have to wait for an opening, I lie,
Wait for that monthly space. While Daddy
Looks out the window at the empty parking lot.

*

I tell my sister about Mom's hands pressing across
My breasts. Her desire not to get dressed.

Oh, God, she'll probably open her robe soon,
Present sagging breasts as twin debutantes,
Those radiant full faces, unaware
Of their stunning power as they descend
Into a gathering crowd.

*

You girls have asked for this.

Her tone of voice. Those surly raised eyebrows.
Lips tight in disapproval, an expression I've earned before.

Don't get clever with me. You aren't
Getting any of my money. I'll hire the best
Lawyer around. You'll see.

Something flicks, changes moods.

You're a good girl.

*

He persists, When do I get my car?

He wants to putt a little and swing a club, or drive to church
Or drive anywhere. Anywhere.

I decide to tell the truth.
Never.
He looks at me and nods
As if he expected this revelation.

*

Daddy, how I wish there was something that could help.
I know this is hard for you.
After a long silence he says,
You know, sometimes the snow falls so fast,
There's no sense shoveling till it stops.

5.

Outside the window of the plane
All is white.

Sights and smells seep
Into a frightening collage.

Sudden death.
An avalanche of snow.

I can't remember
My mother's face, but she is marveling,
   Why, this furniture is exactly like mine.

It *is* yours, Daddy explains.

   Exactly like mine, she persists, as she looks
Around the cheery room. *Somebody chose
The same table, the same lamp, the same chair,*

   And look, flowers. I like roses too.

White spongy hair crystalizes
Around the face
Of a woman saying help, help.
I swallow a gag of remembered peas.

Where are we going? asks a voice in my head.

ADJUSTMENT

Late afternoons Mother wanders
the corridors of the nursing home.
She looks for a way out
to a place where she
can recognize herself.

She's gone from her narrow kitchen
once brightened with pink Formica
where she stood for hours in front
of her old gas stove, satisfied
stirring stews or soups, roasting chickens.

Now she can't boil water, the simplest
of tasks. She spends her days wandering
through rooms of other patients,
filling a shopping bag with treasures—
someone's pair of cheap earrings, a borrowed
polyester dress two sizes too large, a terrycloth
robe with tears at the hem. The nurses and I
laugh when she tells us she's tired,
having spent the day *shopping*.

But late at night I can't laugh
when she grows restless again
and is walking the corridors. She
and the others pass each other
again and again trapped like fish
in this waterless bowl. Outside
are flowers and a bench in the garden
where she's not allowed to go.

Each night she re-hides her purse
in a new spot under the mattress,
packs earrings, a dress and a robe
in her pillowcase, ready for her escape.
I know she's standing by the phone
but can't remember anyone's number.

INSTRUCTIONS
TO THE NIGHT NURSE

Disregard infidelity.
The healing effects of love are proven.

Encourage thievery.
The trying on and keeping of belongings of others
brings great joy.

Praise the persistent woman for her strength.
She repeatedly breaks a window and pushes out
into the night. The garden gate's secure.

Recognize swearing and violent arms and legs
are merely a ghost that comes and goes.
Physical gestures are self-validation
and do not require response.

Accept madness.
Only laughter can guide you through the night.

THE OLD MAN

circles, circles
in aimless procession
all summer across the yard
mowing grass
and sidewalk daily

in the fall
whisk, whisking
invisible dust from one
street corner to the next

his wrinkled skin
clings
to cold bones

he busies himself
like a balloon

exhausting a last twist of air

THE OLD WOMAN

brittle and white
dries up on the tiles
like an old bar of soap

she knows she fell
but when is uncertain

the social security check
is her calendar
even the mailman has
no reason yet to suspect
telephone, doors, and woman
silent

inside her head
night is a permanent visitor

her body is like an old idea
perhaps someone
will rediscover her
tomorrow

FOR SALE

They're painting pale blue
over the white of Myrda's house
but actually
it isn't Myrda's house anymore.

She would stand at the screened
door like it was a window
and watch
all late afternoon for her past.

One night it caught up with her
as she stood too long
await
in her bra and ancient bloomers

expecting her unforgotten lover
to sweep her away.
It was the police who carried her off.
Her doorway's empty now

for all us passersby who miss
those wild dark eyes, staring
beyond us, inside
a halo of spongy white hair.

I liked Myrda's house white.

HUMAN CLOCKS

Ever present time continues
not a linear dart but an
endless circle. Only we are
changing, growing old, human clocks
amidst eternity. She is
the mother nursing all at once:
moonwalkers, Neanderthal man,
Renaissance artists, Medieval
warriors, babes, and the senile.

One old man grasps eternity
in his skull; he is happy and
productive despite the wormlike
veins crawling on his hands,
deep trenches on his hairless brow.

"Time is a tromp l'oeil to ignore,"
he warns. But the young never hear.
The new babes cry out to suckle,
to hurry to grow, but please not
to die. "Let time stand still," they cry.
"But it is," answers the old man.

4

STRANGER

He phoned her out of need
for himself not for her need

but for his need for her to know
his need was overflowing like a backed-up

toilet, everything coming up and over
with no shut-off valve, upheaval that would

never be over, would keep running and
running for the rest of his life. His

need for her to know what he knew so
he phoned and came over bringing

photos, photos he shot himself and
they came out good, photos of

his pretty wife and *her* husband
kissing in a parking lot, kissing

leaning up against a tree, kissing.
Kissing, that's the part she comprehends

but that man in the photo, how can it be!
What else does she not know?

WAKING UP

*"Awake o sleeper,
and arise from the dead . . ."*
—Ephesians 5:14

Their knot loosened so gradually
she never noticed. It slipped away like silk.

Going through motions, indifferent,
detached. With closed eyes

nothing need change, nothing chanced.
Day and night, it was easier to sleep,

pull up a white sheet and slip
into deep currents

washing toward a ledge
of sharp shells. Her cry for help

unheard. Too late
like rising bread that has fallen

or confetti thrown upward
that floats back down. Look.

STUDY IN REEL LIFE

Come back, she calls out the door again
into the black and white day

still the same girl she always was
only now she's fat and frumpy

and Doc is *Daddy*, for the daddy she left behind
and can never go back to, the daddy

who parted with her when she parted her legs
for Doc, who never finished school

so he could support her after she lost
the baby anyway and could never have another.

The old reel repeats its sadness, the slow
suffocation of life—oh, there's action enough

but how can one grow or change, stuck
at the window looking for a little white dog.

Keep busy, the neighbor advises, and she does,
busy dreaming of dancing through her past

while lying on a couch stuck in the present.
She calls out the door again,

lost in a clip of black and white.
Come back.

ADAGIO ADIEU

Together you were seamless,
some smooth sonata in G

he the piano, you the violin,
his strength carrying you

and you always centered,
the main line, and now as I think about it

he definitely the piano, subdued,
his whole life the felt-covered hammers

muted, tender, devoted
to something pure and you

definitely the violin,
holding off at arm's length

never expecting the song
to end like this.

ALCHEMY

Did what you did or didn't
do, cause what he did
and how he did it or

did you not do anything
and he did everything
leaving you

with nothing to do with whatever
he did or didn't do nor
how he dealt with this

and what he has done but
who is responsible
for what parts in all of this

and can it matter to anyone
because isn't there always
forgiveness and of course

some things just happen
and you can still blame but
does there have to be a reason?

STAND-IN

She had a speaking part in this poem,
but after thirty-some years what more
could she say?

At least 1,820 Saturday nights of sex

22,000 dinners

More than 2,000 changes of bed linens

Probably 6,000 towels washed and folded
hung side by side on a shiny chrome bar

Countless socks, T-shirts, boxers, jock straps,
pajamas, jeans, all cleaned and put away and
washed, starched, ironed dress shirts hung
weekly in the closet that still smells of musk

2,000 trips to the bakery, drugstore, shoe repair shop

And vacuuming . . . let's not even go there

But yes, let's be fair, occasionally he sent flowers
and always funny birthday and anniversary cards
(though last year was forgotten)

Several gifts of jewelry, thank you very much

And always, always took out the garbage,
planted the annuals, mowed the lawn
and thank God brought in enough cash
to cover mortgage, doctors, insurance,
food, clothes, braces, and college for the kids

The lawyers will lay it all out, so Your Honor,
we call to the stand: the years.

VARIATIONS

The air is leavened
      The table teems with life

Even if you don't eat it
      The bread, always bread

Upon the table, a glowing slab
      Honey, buttercup, marigold

Unctuous oils   *Give us this day*
      Bountiful and brioche

Sticks, rolls, muffins, loaves,
      Buns seeded, cakes, toast

Slow shapes rising
      Punched down, kneaded

Rise again
      Twisted, knotted, sliced, two-sided

The worth of dough
      Scattered crumbs between us.

PARADELLE FOR A BROKEN HEART

Her love is as a fever longing still.*
Her love is as a fever longing still.
She counts on him to satisfy her needs.
She counts on him to satisfy her needs.
Her fever counts on a love to satisfy.
She is still longing him as her needs.

So many winters pass but this one stays.
So many winters pass but this one stays.
Hope blows away in cold and doors slam shut.
Hope blows away in cold and doors slam shut.
But indoors this one cold stays and blows.
So many winters pass away, slam shut hope.

Of course divorce remains one long cold kiss.
Of course divorce remains one long cold kiss.
Ill-fated wrecks of love grow icy cold.
Ill-fated wrecks of love grow icy cold.
Long divorce remains cold of course.
Cold wrecks grow one icy kiss of ill-fated love.

So her ill-fated love wrecks many winters.
Her longing still counts on him of course.
One kiss of hope is but one long slam.
She needs to satisfy a cold shut away.
Love blows indoors and stays as fever grows.
Divorce remains this icy pass. Cold. Cold.

*Variation on first line of Shakespeare's Sonnet 147

CENTO: SATISFYING THE MUSE

How unusual to be living a life of continual self-expression.
The burden of saying some *thing*.

In the beginning you understand the world but not yourself,
And when you finally understand yourself

You no longer understand the world. Consider yourself
Lucky to have come this far. I must have thought so once

Because I could say the morning died like candle wax
And no one would question its truth.

How much is anyone whose heart speaks for him
Responsible for what his heart has told him?

I celebrate myself, and sing myself . . .
I loafe and invite my soul,

The Soul selects her own Society –
Then – shuts the Door –

I have not been able to eliminate.
And yet—it is the question I keep answering.

ERASURES

After Marcel Broodthaers

At a workshop the nametags say

Hello my name is, so I cover over *Hell*

With a simple stroke, empowered

To change destiny's uncertainty to nonexistence

Then delete *my, n, e* and *is* and part of my name

Transforming with sleight of hand

So it reads *o am Sad*

And suddenly and surprisingly

My mood transforms as well, an exaptation

Of collage with gadgets and tools

Making what was clear, now blurred

The white-outs and paste-overs

Burying words and their meanings

A small funeral of what was to what is

Not absence but change

Like metamorphosis, this butterfly,

As in a store window today where

Mannequins have no faces

Mysterious and magical

Their heads replaced by bunches of flowers.

"FROG-HATTED MAN"

After viewing Michael Lucero's
"Frog-Hatted Man"

One hand steadies his hat.
The other on his heart that really is
a simple house. A door glazed over
in egg-shell blue.

An expressionless
face, a neck blue above a tight bow tie
splotched with yellow and
red that runs down his torso too.

A lawn in front of the house colors
his abdomen green and trickles along
a riverbed of tans to genitalia
exposed where he sits, legs wide,
black with spots and dots
of blue and green.

Over his heart
only the hand looks
familiar, a thumb, four fingers,
white flecked with black lines.

A figure
struts across his back, passing by
as I am, talking to one yellow ear,
one blue, an impossible maze
tattooed on one cheek.

When a door opens, the wind's rush
is enough to swoop any hat
        flip it here
   then there
      as if a frog leaping.

"THE BATHER"

A commissioned Picasso sculpture
completed by Nesjar following
Picasso's death

The lady's bones are made of iron.

But she was not always so: conceived
in Picasso's eye, her folded
cardboard adolescence grew
to 28 feet, a mass of concrete—
her form, smooth
and simple, her childlike pose
belying blood of stone.

To a viewer, she always was.
She had no birth: one day a truck
backed up, deposited her, full-boned.

But many men built her frame,
packed her with black
uniform rock, drilled holes
in her uncomplaining form,
made her a vessel pumped full
of creamy cement, filling her
with permanence,
an immortality dreamed of.

Nesjar stood back and nodded.

Only when they finally disrobed her,
let fall the huge wooden sheets,
did she take command, show the blowtorch
where to find her planned beauty,
reveal her hidden smile.

A 50-ton woman can dazzle.

Now her thick Betograve hair,
dark, mysterious, blows forever
with or without the wind.

"SIX DANCES IN BULGARIAN RHYTHM"

—Bella Bartok's *Mikrokosmos*
For Liz

Her black sequined bodice
            catches and holds light
        falling from a chandelier

            an overture of applause
        igniting performer, audience, music
one blaze of chords
            invasive as smoke

                        empathy rising
        splaying the audience
            to European cities,
                        a taste of seared foie gras,
a thrill of birds flapping near
                the tall leaded-glass window

        thoughts dancing
            over hot coals: the always face of mother,
sparks
        snapping onto nerve stems,
                    the body atremble, eyes
closing on scraps of memory

                scabs picked and bleeding again
        gone in a flash

                    the dazzle of dreams
        fantasy flaring in a blue cloudless sky,
heart pounding full of the world

        and the body singing on the keyboard
            Glorious, Glorious.

"HOG CALLIN' BLUES"

In memory of John Stubblefield

The hogs squeal and squ-eee-a-l
    from the saxophone

        till sweat greases his face
          the flex of his arms

He stops mid-bar to breathe
    shakes his furrowed brow

        a thin spray of surprise
   like a lemon's squirt

hits the rim
    as he inhales with open lips

       jazz juice
        with a lick of salt

           one polyphonic drop

propulsive to next notes
    arching upward

       a peal brutishly sensual
  singing pink in our blood

    with us high on the hog
        comin' home with Mingus singin'

piggety pig, higgety hog, pi-HOG, HOG
    poggity hog, higgity pig, pi-HOG, HOG

MATING DANCE

You
are secretive
as a seahorse
camouflaged in your
bed of sea grass. Don't
think   I am falling for
your charm
holding my hand
with your monkey
tail and
I shall not be your
shrimp, for I too show
some spine, though
I'm aware you are
watching my eyes
as I scoot away.
I have no eggs
to deposit in your
pouch. So stop
changing colors.   I hear
the bones in   your head
click   while you
dance under stars. Leave me
alone or I'll have you dried
and put on a keychain.

I LOVE YOUR DRESS

Love (*luv*) n. v.
1.   *a profoundly tender, passionate
affection for another person, especially
when based on sexual attraction.*

But love isn't only
for another person. I love
myself. I love my dog.
I love today with its cornflower clear sky.
I love writing poetry, words lingering
moist on my tongue
like artichoke hearts so tender
my eyelids close and flutter.

Luckily the driver of the great Lexicon
makes a turn onto a side street,
love and sex entwined in the back seat
morphing
into any physical response
where love can startle.

While the passion of sex
may be quickly over, and
puppy, motherly, or obedient
love may lack passion, I am passionate
as I think of circling your neck with love beads,
tying a scarf around your hips
in a love knot. I feel it
and I've got to say it now,
I *love* your dress.

PRAYER DAILY

O dear God, please hear my prayer.
O Lord, O Lord.

Oh Lord won't you buy me a Mercedes Benz. *

Oh for heaven's sake!
What in the name of God?

Do you hear them giggle and prattle,
"Oh my God . . . oh my Gaaawwd!"?

I'm listening Lord. Don't let me down.
I'm counting on you Lord.

And that flat screen TV would be nice too.
God, it's me. Are you listening?

Holy Mary Mother of God
Pray for us.

Goddammit!
God blew it.

Well God bless you.
And God bless America.

Gesundheit.

God love ya, you're doin' your best.

But it's God-awful! Lordy loo.
Get me out of this godforsaken place.

This is beautiful. It's God's country.

Jesus, Jesus Christ, *Jesus Christo,*
Christ on a crutch.

Riff of celestial song.
Lord, what beauty.

Do you God distinguish
disappointment from disbelief?

Are you godless or godlike?
I'm a godmother, does that count?

I don't give a good goddam.

Holey Moley.
Christ Jesus Mary and Joseph. God help us.
Amen.

God only knows.

God, are you listening?

*Song excerpt from "Mercedes Benz" by Janis Joplin

LIKE NOTHING ELSE

You are so you.
Your eyes sparkle like eyes.
Your lashes, dark long lashes.
Your smile is usually a smile
But sometimes is not a smile.
Your teeth are your teeth.
Your nose juts out like a nose.
Your toes wiggle like toes.
Your hands open like hands.
Your feet dance like feet.
Your back is a back, back there.
Your fanny is not an ass,
Your fanny is a cute fanny.
Your breasts are two breasts,
Both breasts are breasts I like.
Your belly button is not a button,
Your belly button is just a belly button.
Your ankle turns like an ankle.
Your heel is always a heel.
Your elbows bend like elbows.
Your ears are here and hear like ears.
Your heart is more than a heart,
Your heart is both love and machine.
Loved, you look loved.
Your words are like no other words,
Your words give your word.
Your voice sounds
Like something you'd say.
You are so you.

A BURGER,
WITHOUT THE BURGER, PLEASE

For Skye

Waitress thought it a joke,
pencil point on paper,
waiting, still waiting
after the repeat.

Did you ever want the vase
but not the flowers?
The sex but not the man?
The baby but not the birth?
The moon but not the night?

What goes wrong may be oh so right.
Come closer
where I can know you without the light.

THE JOYS OF COOKING

"That which thy fathers have bequeathed to thee,
earn it anew if thou wouldst posses it."
—Goethe: Faust

If we hadn't argued
over the minutes per pound
to roast a stuffed turkey
we might never have turned
to *JOY OF COOKING*

Mistakenly I looked
for GAME in the index,
turned to a short section
and discovered recipes for
woodchuck, beaver, opossum,
bear, raccoon, squirrel,
rabbit, hare . . .

If possible, trap 'possum and feed it
on milk and cereals for 10 days before killing.
No mention of naming pet 'possum
and subsequent pitfalls

Treat as for pig by immersing
the unskinned animal in water . . .
Test frequently by plucking at the hair.
Here I'm plucking at my hair
and shift attention to Peccary
(recognized by his dark gray coat with white collar?)

Immediately after killing, remove the musk glands
in the middle of the back. This meat needs
marinating before cooking.

Killing! Hmmm,
perhaps the woodchuck who ruins my garden?
Dress as for rabbit,
but watch for and remove 7 to 9 small sacs or kernels
in the small of the back and under the forearm.

Forefathers were thoughtful
to bequeath these feasts
(misnomer amidst modern abundance)
first printed in 1931.
And here, in my yellowed 1967 edition,
I realize the importance of friendship

if I want to cook a bear.
remove all fat at once,
as it turns rancid very quickly;
(reminiscent of failed solitary efforts
of Christopher McCandless "Into the Wild")

And I hope one of my friends is a hunter,
someone who knows not to carry game
on a hot car radiator, but ties it to the roof,
cruising back home as cool as the evening

One who knows how to select a young pheasant,
one whose spur at back of foot is pliable and has rounded end

Or a friend who recognizes a great partridge,
one with a breastbone that breaks easily when bent
and a leg bone that's plump and round near the foot

And if I am ever in possession of a beaver,
I now know I can eat its tail.
Hold over open flame until rough skin blisters.
Remove from heat. When cool, peel off skin.
Roast over coals or simmer until tender

No doubt Goethe would've agreed
to accept culinary advice
without philosophical analysis
and would've selected a quick sauce for furred game
and certainly he could appreciate
the romance of selecting
a certain someone to share
a roasted feast under the light of a full moon

And just so you know the wisdom
I've gleaned, look out your window:
Gray squirrels are preferred;
red ones are small and quite gamey in flavor.
But the best advice that still holds true:
There are, proverbially, many ways to skin a squirrel.

THE WRONG E

I've been informed by the esteemed *Journal*
that I'm taking the wrong Vitamin E,

not the one with gamma-tocopherol
but the one with alpha-tocopherol, her weak sister.

Does this mean that my body
has been fed the wrong messages?

Have I been given the E of foreign languages,
with accents acute or grave, or perhaps circumflex,

those tiny diacritical marks blocking my arteries,
causing a traffic jam of sorts for all of the other

letters of the alphabet swimming in my blood?
And what about all those other letters,

could I be taking the wrong C
or the wrong A or D?

I do feel confident I must be taking
the right Bs—they're all numbered

but what if those friends B1, B6 and B12
pal around with the wrong E

and create some kind of trouble
in my body; in fact, excuse me for a moment

I'm not feeling so well just now,
probably something I ate,

all these letters, all these numbers
swirling inside me,

hitting my stomach
bold as a salami from the corner Deli

with its sign that flashes "You're number is up"
and an arrow pointing to the exit.

LIFE

In memory of Karl Shapiro

. . . Crunch! Crush! Crunch!
Pass me some LIFE.

Just like the spoon shouldn't be an issue,
it goes beyond the grain. Then
there's which milk—
2%, 1%, skim, whole, lactose-free, soybean—
and the selection of bowl
even if it's the same every day.

Open the box from the top.
You can be a purist.
Bowl by bowl, day by day,
you'll reach the prize.

Or open the box from the bottom.
Get to the prize first.

No bowl can encompass all of life.

Get real. This is LIFE.
Dump the cereal.
Take the prize.
Leave the empty box for someone else.

From the despair of an empty bowl
comes the clang of a spoon.

ORANGE

The word dangles like a speckled fish. *Orange.*
The spelling word in Miss Dade's second grade class.
Or is it *o-a-r-a-n-g-e* or *o-a-r-n-g-e?*
I can never remember.

The word could be a moon of fall harvest
Or vegetables carefully planted months before

Or a river, or a town, or a destination somewhere between.

Not red. Nor yellow

But a thought
Like fruit's
Juicy bursts through a wedge of membrane—
If only I could hold those curved pieces together,
Keep it whole in my clenched fist.

I print firmly with a Number 2 pencil
On the shellacked desktop of wood,
Orange etched properly in my mind as well,
A blank paper ready for dictation in Room 204.

When she collects the tests she stands beside my desk,
All ten words correct on my wide-ruled lines
Still covering an unused lie.

Triumph flaps like wings of a caged colorful bird.

STANDARD QUESTIONS
(AT THE READING)

Anytime, anywhere

Actually, mornings

Iced soy chai

(Laughter) Hardly;
Sometimes for months

No one. Well, Kinnell, Collins,
Adonizzio, Olds, Pinsky

Yes, well, they're dead, but Coleridge, Emerson, Bishop

Like all art forms, man is a domino

I've never noticed that

Are you sure? . . . I'm from Nebraska

17 drafts; plucking perfect words

Perhaps growing up embarrassed
I couldn't eat hamburger pizza on Fridays

A dialogue between
What's happened and what may
From poet to poet to receptive ear

That's true. Few
Poems see print
Competing with Whitman and Stafford,
Posthumous (OED?) feet

On the threshold
Inspires one to get larger shoes
And never die on the beach

Lasting of course
I never eat tuna in my poems

WRITING LESSON

For Bobbykins

First you *gots* to learn to dance

Stand up man
                    Feel the beat

Your dick
            finds the way
                        like a tongue

        for the ear
                    or a tongue
                            for the eye

Till your *feets*
            show the beat
                        My man

Words will sing
            as the hips
                        pluck the notes

From the air
            loose 'n cool

Ride
        it
                    down

BITE

across the empty street
            howling

Hey fox
        you're lookin'
            g-o-o-o-o-o-d

    asphalt
dark as blood

                words slice
                        deep

                    Damn right
        at the cross-
walk

        nose tip toward the moon

            a closed
                smile
            conceals

        teeth
            edgy
        as
    night

HOMAGE TO THE TYPEWRITER

After "Hommage" by Leopoldo M. Maler
from The Hess Art Collection, Napa, CA

Someone has sent me a postcard with a picture
Of a burning Underwood Standard Typewriter.
Golden flames rise out of the black carriage
As if the words typed, so hot and intense,

Burn in spontaneous combustion.
I love this old familiar machine,
The shiny black Underwood with its wide, open smile,
The type bars ready to rise and engage with a press

On any of its four rows of golden keys. The basic
Numbers two through nine followed by a zero
On the top row, then the second row of keys
With its familiar *Y* in the middle, always

Keeping the keyboard centered on a basic question.
I love the way you can cover the whole alphabet
With just the little finger of the left hand, shifting
From *A* to *Z*, hands poised like a pianist's

Over the memorized keyboard. Words
Engaging the orderly letters, one at a time,
Stand ready to divulge the answers to whatever
Burning questions of prior wordsmiths.

Now this beloved antiquity rests
As forerunner of the contemporary computer
On which we can no longer throw a carriage,
Nor even, at the end of the line, ring a tiny bell.

COVER LETTER

In memory of Ryan Caster

Dear Ms. Oates:

and does eat oats
Thank you for your comment
and little lambs eat ivy, a kid'll eat I've

even enjoyed yet another issue,
especially the most recent with
Tom Wayman's *"Messages"*

was *he that last hangup call*
so I want to send you something
about another teacher who admired

Tom's work, especially that poem
when he gets the girl into bed
but is joined by Doctors Marx and Freud

making Ryan laugh to assuage fears of commitment
and wanting to read the poem at a wedding
reception to quell ceremonial anxieties

which turned out to be his anxieties
and no one else's so that's worth a laugh too
but a *lifelong* commitment—how can we be *sure*

so he left the poem at home, quoting
Ruth Fainlight's *Fire* instead, saying
Love like fire is worth the risk

121

A POEM IS MY DONKEY

It carries anything and everything

Once it carried a ten-year-old boy
     from the path of an oncoming van
          to a sparkle of light caught in evergreen

Often it carries silence
     picking its way over rough terrain

Other times, its sides heave
     in a rush of wind and lightning
        the eye of a storm

It carries me to the edge of the world
     where I fly with eagles

Sometimes it slips but uses words
     to carry me up and over

Then circles and circles
     kicking up dust

Eyes of flickering light
     showing me what I cannot see

PARKING LOT SPECTACLE
(WITH COLLOQUIALISMS)

A voice calls out,

What day is this?

Sunday.

But it can't be, she says,

I just had Monday.

We believe her this weekend

and wish her, *Good Tuesday*

and drive on home for a fine roast beef Sunday.

At dinner on Wednesday we wonder

like bread soaks up milk, could Thursday be thirsty

and which fish shall we Friday?

And please don't be Sadder-day,

Cheer up.

When Sunday shines again and drops

into the lot, a ray astray on ashen,

we all rive away.

Have a good day.

Ta tah.

WHAT DOES IT TAKE?

One that struts naked across the page
embarrassing
you not me? Dark tips alert
before chiaroscuro shadows?
Fireworks? A dancing horse?
A clear peal of bells from across the mountain
as a rooster crows? A hummingbird
flaring abreast at your window?
What if all fragile things
were pressed in a vise? *Tick. Tock.*
I mean you.
Don't run away.
There's no alligator behind you.

HIGH COO-COO

An egg cannot fly
though the bird within trembles
possibility

Notes

"An Intimacy of Matter" was composed in memory of our beloved family pet for 16 years, Brecon, a Welsh terrier. Our experience has helped others gain solace after such a loss.

"The Bather" is a 28-foot tall cement sculpture by Pablo Picasso commissioned for the grounds of Gould Corporation, Rolling Meadows, Illinois. After Picasso died, his assistant Nesjar completed the installation. Many years later the sculpture was returned to France.

"Cento: Satisfying the Muse" uses a poetic form from the 3rd or 4th century that is a poem composed of odd fragments like a quilt entirely made up of lines by others. The sources for this poem include Billy Collins, "Foundling"; Dawn Lundy Martin, "Our Wandering"; Mary Ruefle, "Little Golf Pencil"; Adrienne Rich, "Endpapers"; Louise Gluck, "Afterword"; Major Jackson, "Why I Write Poetry"; Mark Jarman, "George W. Bush"; Walt Whitman, "Song of Myself"; Emily Dickinson, "The Soul selects her own Society"; Tony Hoagland, "Wrong Question."

"Cover Letter" was composed in memory of Ryan Caster, a brilliant high school English teacher who attended our daughter's wedding and was killed in a motorcycle/vehicle accident a few days later while on holiday. A week later I received a lengthy poetic letter from him that he must have mailed before his holiday in which he contemplated both love and marriage. He questioned, How do we marry when we understand that we continually grow and change thoughout our lives? How can we be sure? How can we keep a candle lit and upright? With no way to answer his letter or thank him for his insights or assuage his fears of commitment, I wrote this poem to remember that at age 23, he was gone, like fire and light, a brilliance extinguished.

"Frog-Hatted Man" was composed after viewing Michael Lucero's colorful sculpture, "Frog-Hatted Man," 1991, The Mint Museum of Craft and Design, Charlotte, North Carolina.

"Hog Callin' Blues" was written after attending a performance by the renowned John Stubblefield on the saxophone with Mingus Big Band in New York City.

"Homage to the Typewriter" was inspired by sculpture, "Homage" by Leopoldo M. Maler, 1974, 10 ½" x 19 ¼" x 12 ⅜", part of the Hess Collection Winery, Napa, California.

"Krabloonik Restaurant" was inspired by Krabloonik Restaurant in Snowmass, Colorado.

"Mastering the MRI" references Uma Thurman's performance in the movie "Kill Bill."

"Mating Dance" was inspired by a special exhibit of the vast variety of seahorses from around the world at the Monterey Aquarium, Monterey, California, where seahorse keychains were for sale in the gift shop.

"Reprisal: *'the knives and the herring'*" references *A Season in Hell* by French poet Arthur Rimbaud who had a violent relationship with his lover Paul Verlain.

"Study in Reel Life" references the movie, "Come Back Little Sheba."

"Thirteen Ways of Looking at the Sea" is patterned after "Thirteen Ways of Looking at a Blackbird" by Wallace Stevens, from *The Collected Poems* of Wallace Stevens, copyright 1923.

"Writing Lesson" is in memory of artist Robert Natkin who one evening leapt from our dinner table to explain how writing and art come from within.

ACKNOWLEDGMENTS

Grateful acknowledgment is made to the editors of the following literary magazines, in which some of the poems in this book were first published, as well as to the judges and selection panels for the awards some of these poems received.

"Adjustment," "Circles," "If Lights Dim" and "The Clock Shoe": first appeared in *Prairie Schooner.*

"Adjustment," "Circles" and "The Clock Shoe": a group of poems that received the Hugh J. Luke Poetry Award, 1996, from *Prairie Schooner.*

"The Clock Shoe": selected for the anthology *Best of Prairie Schooner* (University of Nebraska Press, 2001) celebrating the magazine's 75th anniversary.

"An Intimacy of Matter": selected as a finalist in the 2001 Poetry Competition sponsored by *Inkwell;* first appeared in *Hope Whispers.*

"Balloon": first appeared in *AJN, American Journal of Nursing.*

"High Coo-Coo": selected for a harpsichord composition by Elizabeth Lauer.

"Human Clocks": selected for *Dial-A-Poem, Chicago!*

"I Love Your Dress": a finalist for *The Look of Love* 2007 Poetry Award from The Northwest Cultural Council, Barrington, Illinois.

"Krabloonik Restaurant": first appeared in *Rhino.*

"Letter to Cambodian Faces": first appeared in *Colere.*

"No Return," and "Onion Evenings": first appeared in *The Midwest Quarterly.*

"Onion Evenings," "The Clock Shoe," "No Return" and "Revelation": translated for the website "Russian Globe" Literary Magazine.

"Orange": awarded First Honorable Mention, Free Verse, Poets & Patrons Contest, 1990.

"Peter": first appeared in *Whetstone*.

"Postcard From Harbour Island, Bahamas": first appeared in *Arts Alive: A Literary Review*.

"Revelation": first appeared in *Willow Review*.

"Snake Love": finalist for a Randall Jarrell Poetry Prize, 1996.

"Standard Questions (At the Reading)": first appeared in *Thema*.

"Traveler": first appeared in *Arts Alive: A Literary Review*.

"The Joys of Cooking": first appeared in *What's Cooking*.

"The Logic of Snow": awarded Honorable Mention in the XVIII *New Millennium Writing Awards;* first appeared in *Trajectory*.

"Vestige": selected by Slapering Hol Press Reading Series of Poets and Writers on War and Peace at Hudson Valley Writer's Center.

Grateful thanks to those who have taken an interest in my poems and encouraged the creative process. With special thanks:

To the memory of Karl Shapiro, for providing my earliest encouragement while at the University of Nebraska to write and rewrite, and to narrow my lens, and for giving me my first opportunity to serve as co-editor of his 212 Club, writing class literary magazine.

To the memory of my mentor and arts advocate Flo Bash, founder of Barrington Area Arts Council, Barrington, Illinois, who once asked me to write a poem with "a purple rim across the bay."

To Barrington Writers' Workshop members who offered helpful critiques, especially dear friends Marsha Portnoy and Jean Tolle for perpetual support.

To Kathy Umlauf, founder and director of Northwest Cultural Council, Barrington, Illinois, who has spent her life championing the arts.

To Greenwich Pen Women for camaraderie and inspiration amongst artistes.

To Dennis Wyszynski for photography of the cover art.

To my husband, Brian, for a lifetime of shared experiences and adventures, and for his support and nurturing of my creative spirit.

To my daily amazement of the complexity of humanity and the wonders of nature that makes me whisper, "I see you God."

To Muse Ink Press for publication and to Joanne Dearcopp for her invaluable expertise, guidance and support.

To my readers, known and unknown, for breathing life into my words on the page. This book is for you.

ABOUT THE AUTHOR

Sandra Berris was born in Chicago, but grew up in Lincoln, Nebraska. Her degrees are from the University of Nebraska and Stanford University. She was co-founder and co-editor of *Whetstone*, a literary magazine that garnered eleven National Endowment for the Arts/Illinois Arts Council literary awards as well as a 1995 American Literary Magazine Award for editorial excellence during its eighteen years. Her poems have appeared in many little magazines and she was a recipient of *Prairie Schooner's* Hugh J. Luke Poetry Prize. Her work was anthologized in *Best of Prairie Schooner* (University of Nebraska Press, 2001). She lives in Carmel by the Sea, California.

CPSIA information can be obtained
at www.ICGtesting.com
Printed in the USA
BVOW09s1436241117
501091BV00012B/1212/P